DATE DUE

First
Facts™

Health Matters

Obesity

by Jason Glaser

Consultant:
James R. Hubbard, MD
Fellow in the American Academy of Pediatrics
Iowa Medical Society
West Des Moines, Iowa

Capstone
press®

Mankato, Minnesota

First Facts is published by Capstone Press,
151 Good Counsel Drive, P.O. Box 669, Mankato, Minnesota 56002.
www.capstonepress.com

Library of Congress Cataloging-in-Publication Data
Glaser, Jason.
    Obesity / by Jason Glaser.
    p. cm.—(First facts. Health matters)
    Summary: "Describes obesity, how and why it occurs, and how to treat and prevent it"—
Provided by publisher.
    Includes index.
    ISBN-13: 978-0-7368-6331-5 (hardcover)
    ISBN-10: 0-7368-6331-1 (hardcover)
    1. Obesity—Juvenile literature. I. Title. II. Series.
RC628.G55 2007
616.3'98—dc22
                                             2006002832

Editorial Credits:
Shari Joffe, editor; Biner Design, designer; Juliette Peters, set designer; Jo Miller, photo researcher;
    Scott Thoms, photo editor

Photo Credits:
Art Directors/Spencer Grant, 19
Corbis/Richard Hutchings, cover (foreground); Tom & Dee Ann McCarthy, 18; zefa/Ronnie
    Kaufman, 15
Getty Images Inc./Stone/Donna Day, 8-9; Taxi/Arthur Tilley, 10-11
PhotoEdit Inc./Bob Daemmrich, 6; Jonathan Nourok, 13; Mark Richards, 12
Photo Researchers, Inc./Coneyl Jay, 17; Gusto, 5; Phanie, 14
Shutterstock/Max Blain, 1
U.S. Department of Agriculture, 21
Visuals Unlimited/Dr. Fred Hossler, cover (background), 20

1 2 3 4 5 6 11 09 08 07 06

Table of Contents

Signs of Obesity

Each time you run, you get tired, breathe harder, and get sore knees. Your clothes feel very tight, even though you haven't gotten taller. Your brother tells you that you snore at night. Sometimes you wake up because you can't breathe well. These are warning signs of obesity.

Fact!
Obesity is not a disease. It is an unhealthy condition.

What Is Obesity?

Your body gets energy from food. This energy is measured in **calories**. Sometimes people take in more calories than they need. The body stores extra calories as fat. If this goes on over a long time, a person can become very overweight, or obese. People with obesity have more body fat than is healthy.

Fact!
Extra calories are stored in fat cells. Over time, kids who take in too many calories get more and bigger fat cells.

How Does Obesity Happen?

Obesity may happen when kids eat too many calories and aren't active enough. Many kids eat junk food, which is high in fat and sugar. They may spend too much time in front of the computer or television.

Obesity sometimes runs in families. So some kids may have to work harder to keep extra weight off.

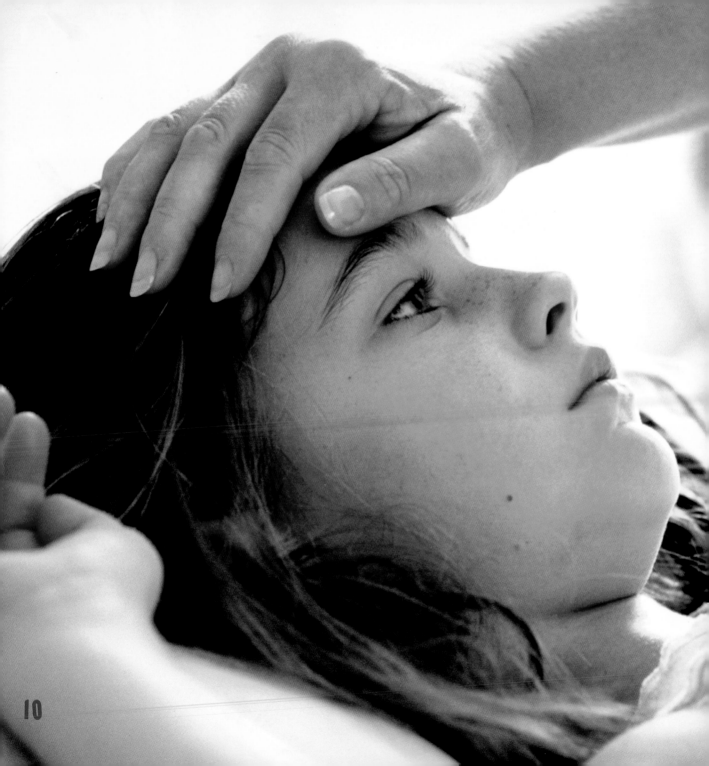

What Else Could It Be?

Signs of obesity can be signs of other things. Illnesses like the flu can cause lack of energy. Children with **asthma** sometimes have trouble breathing. They may not be able to exercise for long periods. Kids with large **tonsils** may have trouble breathing while sleeping.

Should Kids See a Doctor?

A doctor can test for obesity by comparing your weight to your height. Tests can be run to see if your weight is putting too much **stress** on your heart.

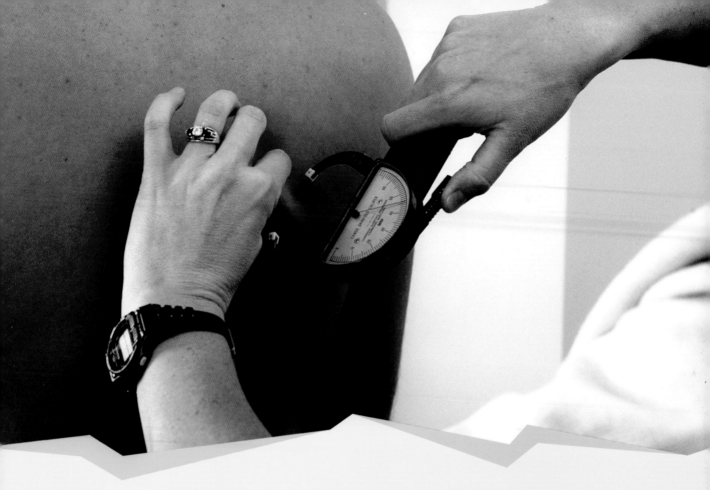

Doctors can also measure how much of your body is fat and how much is muscle. They can pinch your skin with **calipers** to see how much fat is under it.

Treatment

In most cases, obesity can be treated. Doctors usually suggest a diet of healthy, low-fat foods. Smaller **portions** may help, too.

Overweight kids usually need to change their exercise habits as well. Walking, karate, and biking are good activities. They burn off fat but are easy on the heart.

What Happens Without Treatment?

Carrying extra weight is hard on the body. The heart has to work harder to pump blood. Being obese can lead to heart problems later in life. Kids with obesity are also more likely to get **diabetes**. This disease prevents people's bodies from turning food into energy. Kids must then control their diets. They may also have to take pills or shots of medicine.

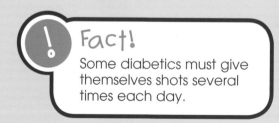

Fact!
Some diabetics must give themselves shots several times each day.

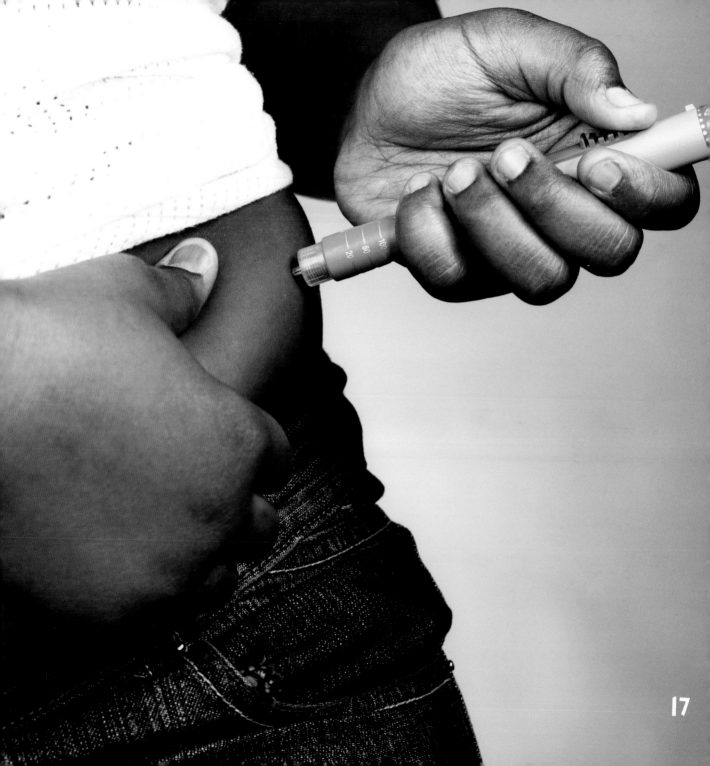

Ways to Prevent Obesity

Good eating habits can prevent obesity. Eat a balanced diet that includes lots of fruits and vegetables. Limit high-fat foods and sugary drinks.

Getting enough exercise can also
prevent obesity. Jumping rope, swimming,
and team sports are good ways to keep
fit and strengthen the heart.

Amazing but True!

Once you are past **puberty**, you can't gain or lose fat cells. But you can still lose weight. Each fat cell can shrink or grow larger. With plenty of exercise and a healthy diet, fat cells will shrink.

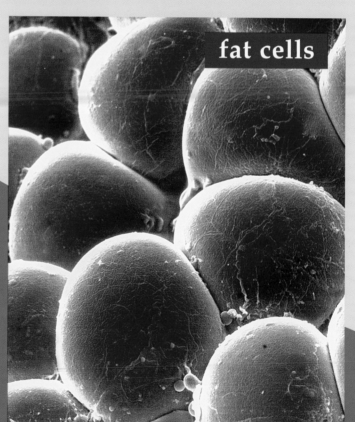

fat cells

Hands On: Food Guide Pyramid

The U.S. government's Food Guide Pyramid helps kids understand how to eat healthy and avoid obesity. The six colored stripes represent the five different food groups, plus oils. Every day, kids need to eat foods from each group. The different widths of the stripes reminds kids that they should eat more from some food groups than others.

What You Need
Large poster board
Orange, green, red,
  yellow, blue, purple,
  and black markers

What You Do
1. On the poster board, draw a large pyramid, using the illustration on this page as a guide.
2. Inside the pyramid, color in the stripes that represent the food groups.
3. Every day for a week, use a black marker write down each food you eat in the striped area where it belongs.
4. At the end of the week, you'll see if you've been eating healthy!

For more information on healthy eating habits, go to
http://www.MyPyramid.gov/kids/

21

Glossary

asthma (AZ-muh)—a condition that causes a person to wheeze and have difficulty breathing

calipers (KAL-ih-puhrs)—a device that has arms used to measure thickness

calorie (KAL-uh-ree)—a measurement of the amount of energy that food gives you

diabetes (dye-uh-BEE-teez)—a disease in which there is too much sugar in the blood

portion (POR-shuhn)—a part of something

puberty (PYOO-bur-tee)—the time when a person's body changes from a child's to an adult's

stress (STRESS)—strain or pressure

tonsils (TON-suhlz)—flaps of soft tissue that lie on each side of the throat

Read More

Feeney, Kathy. *Get Moving: Tips on Exercise.* Your Health. Mankato, Minn.: Bridgestone Books, 2002.

Royston, Angela. *What Should We Eat?* Stay Healthy! Chicago: Heinemann Library, 2006.

Scott, Janine. *The Food Pyramid.* Spyglass Books. Minneapolis: Compass Point Books, 2003.

Internet Sites

FactHound offers a safe, fun way to find Internet sites related to this book. All of the sites on FactHound have been researched by our staff.

Here's how:

1. Visit *www.facthound.com*

2. Choose your grade level.

3. Type in this book ID **0736863311** for age-appropriate sites. You may also browse subjects by clicking on letters, or by clicking on pictures and words.

4. Click on the **Fetch It** button.

FactHound will fetch the best sites for you!

Index